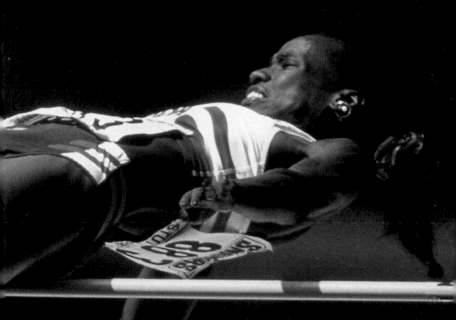

ATHLETICS
FIELD
by Jason Page

**JUMPING
FOR JOY-NER**
In the 1988 Olympic heptathlon,
Jackie Joyner-Kersee (USA) smashed
her own world record by
76 points.

W9-ABU-020

FIELD EVENTS

This book contains everything you need to know about field events and their Olympic history, plus the full lowdown on the modern pentathlon and triathlon.

TRACK & FIELD

Athletic events are grouped together in two categories. Running races are known as track events. These include sprints, hurdles, relays, and medium- and long-distance races. Events that involve throwing or jumping are called field events, and it's these that we'll be looking at in detail in this book.

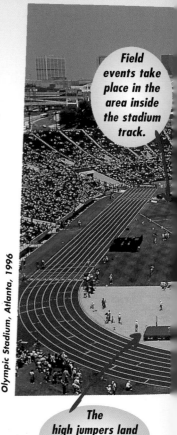

Field events take place in the area inside the stadium track.

Olympic Stadium, Atlanta, 1996

The high jumpers land on a cushioned bed!

SUPER STATS

Around 3.5 billion people are expected to watch the 2000 Olympics in Sydney on television. If everyone in the entire audience held hands, they could circle the Earth more than 10 times!

SOMETHING OLD, SOMETHING NEW

The modern pentathlon has its roots in the ancient Olympic Games. The triathlon, on the other hand, is a new sport. It will be included in the Games for the very first time at the Sydney Olympics in 2000.

RAY-MARKABLE!

Between 1900 and 1908, an American athlete named Ray Ewry won 10 gold medals in three different jumping events. That's more than anyone else has ever won in any Olympic sport!

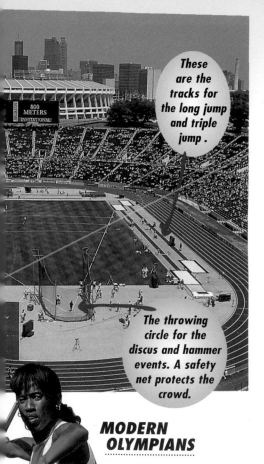

These are the tracks for the long jump and triple jump.

The throwing circle for the discus and hammer events. A safety net protects the crowd.

OLYMPICS FACT FILE

The Olympic Games were first held in Olympia, Greece, about 3,000 years ago. They took place every four years until they were abolished in A. D. 393.

A Frenchman named Pierre de Coubertin (1863–1937) revived the Games, and the first modern Olympics were held in Athens in 1896.

The modern Games have been held every four years since 1896, except in 1916, 1940, and 1944, because of war. Special 10th-anniversary Games took place in 1906.

The symbol of the Olympic Games is five interlocking colored rings. Together, they represent the five different continents from which athletes come to compete.

MODERN OLYMPIANS

The Olympics have changed a great deal since the first modern Games were held in 1896. One of the biggest changes has been the number of female athletes taking part. When the Olympics come to Sydney, women will compete in several events for the first time — including the pole vault, the hammer, the triathlon, and the modern pentathlon!

HIGH JUMP

To have a chance of winning a medal, Olympic high jumpers have to leap more than 7 feet (2 meters) into the air. That's like jumping over the top of your front door!

THREE STRIKES & YOU'RE OUT!

High jumpers are allowed three attempts at each jump. Those who get over the crossbar without knocking it down, go on to the next round of the competition. Those who don't, are knocked out. In each round, the bar is raised at least 1 inch (2 cm) higher. Whoever manages to clear the highest jump, wins.

DID YOU KNOW?

High jumpers are allowed to touch the crossbar as they jump over it. However, if the bar falls down, the jump doesn't count.

In the event of a tie (when two athletes have jumped the same height), the gold medal is awarded to the one who has knocked down the crossbar the fewest times.

Dora Ratjen (GER) came in fourth in the women's high jump in 1936. However, this athlete was later disqualified when it was discovered that "she" was actually a man in disguise!

Charles Austin

SHAPE UP

Olympic athletes come in all shapes and sizes. Top high jumpers such as Charles Austin (USA), who won gold at the 1996 Olympic Games, tend to be tall and thin with long legs.

MEN'S RECORDS: WORLD: Javier Sotomayor (CUB) 8.04 ft (2.45m). **OLYMPIC:** Charles Austin (USA) 7.84 f

ANIMAL OLYMPIANS

The high jump champ of the animal kingdom is a small African antelope called the klipspringer. Springy by name and springy by nature, the klipspringer can leap 24.6 feet (7.5 meters) into the air. That's more than three times the human high jump record!

HAPPY LANDINGS

The rules state that high jumpers must take off from one foot, not two. To help them leap as high as possible, they are allowed to run during their takeoff for as long or as short as they like. A soft landing bed is placed on the other side of the jump to prevent them from injuring themselves when they land.

Dick Fosbury

WHAT A FLOP!

In the 1968 Olympic Games, a high jumper named Dick Fosbury (USA) caused a sensation by jumping over the bar backward! Until Fosbury came along, high jumpers had always jumped forward, landing facedown on the mat. Fosbury's revolutionary technique won him the gold medal. Almost all Olympic high jumpers use his method, which is known as the "Fosbury Flop."

SAND PITS

Long jumpers land in a pit filled with soft sand.
The sand helps to break their fall so that the athletes don't injure themselves. It also shows how
far they jumped. Each jump is measured from the
edge of the takeoff board to the nearest mark
made in the sand by the jumper's body.

CLOSE TO THE EDGE

Long jumpers are allowed to run on
their takeoff but they are not
allowed to tread beyond the
white takeoff board. Along the
edge of this board is a line of
soft putty. If an athlete steps
over the edge, a mark will be
made in the putty, and the jump
will not be counted.

DID YOU KNOW?

)) If the judge next to
the takeoff board
raises a red flag, it means
the athlete stepped over
the board, and the jump
does not count. If the
judge raises a white flag,
the jump was OK.

)) The long jump was
one of the original
events in the ancient
Olympic Games.

)) Unlike modern ath-
letes, ancient Roman
and Greek competitors
were allowed to swing
special weights made of
stone or lead to help
them jump farther.

OLYMPIC GOLDEN BOY

Carl Lewis (USA) is one
of the greatest athletes
of all time. At the 1996
Games, he won the long
jump for the fourth time
in a row. But that's
not all. Victories in the
100 meters, 200 meters,
and 400-meter relay
mean that this sports
superstar has nine golds
and one silver
in his Olympic medal
collection.

Carl Lewis

LONG JUMP

To help them leap long distances, long jumpers need a really fast takeoff. So it's not surprising that one of the greatest Olympic long jumpers is also a champion sprinter!

Bob Beamon

JUMPING INTO THE RECORD BOOKS

Long jumper Bob Beamon (USA) leapt into Olympic history during the 1968 Games in Mexico with an incredible jump measuring 29.2 feet (8.9 meters). Beamon's jump shattered the world record of 27.39 feet (8.35 meters) held by Ralph Boston (USA) and set an Olympic record that stands to this day.

ANIMAL OLYMPIANS

The common flea can jump more than a foot (33 cm). That's 220 times the length of its own body. If humans could do that, we'd be able to leap about 416 yards (380 meters). That's more than four times the length of a football field!

WOMEN'S RECORDS: WORLD: Galina Chistyakova (URS) 24.67 ft (7.52m). **OLYMPIC:** Jackie Joyner-Kersee (USA) 24.28 ft (7.40m).

TRIPLE JUMP

*T*he triple jump is three jumps in one. Winning gold in this event takes balance and agility, as well as power.

GOLDEN GIRL

In 1996, Inessa Kravets (UKR) became the first female triple jumper to win an Olympic gold medal. This picture was taken in 1995 at the World Championships, where she broke the women's world record.

ANIMAL OLYMPIANS

Gold medal in the triple jump at the Animal Olympics goes to the South African sharp-nosed frog. One frog, named Santjie, managed to cover 33.79 feet (10.3 meters) in three leaps during a frog race in May 1977. That record still hasn't been broken!

Inessa Kravets

MEN'S RECORDS: WORLD: Jonathan Edwards (GBR) 60.01 ft (18.29m). **OLYMPIC:** Kenny Harrison (USA) 59.35 ft (18.09m).

VIKTOR'S VICTORIES

The most successful Olympic triple jumper ever was Viktor Saneyev (URS). He competed in every Olympic Games from 1968 to 1980, winning three gold medals in a row and a silver. If there had been a prize for making silly faces, it looks like he would have won that as well!

Viktor Saneyev

HOP, STEP, & JUMP

The triple jump is similar to the long jump. But instead of one mighty leap, triple jumpers have to do three! The first is a hop (landing on the same foot they took off from), the second is a step (landing on the other foot), and the third is a jump (landing feet-first in the sand pit).

BALANCING ACT

Watch closely and you'll notice how triple jumpers swing their arms during the final part of the jump. This helps them keep their balance as they fly through the air.

DID YOU KNOW?

The men's triple jump has been part of the Olympic Games since 1896, but women weren't allowed to compete in the event until 1996—100 years later!

James Connolly (USA) became the first modern Olympic champion when he won the triple jump in 1896.

But Connolly would have been disqualified at the Sydney Olympics because he took two hops and a jump instead of a hop, step, and jump. (That was legal in 1896.)

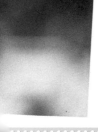

DID YOU KNOW?

Pole vaulters jump more than 20 feet (6 meters) into the air. That's like leaping over a giraffe!

Competitors are allowed to tape the pole to improve their grip and to protect the end of the pole.

The Olympic record for the pole vault at the first Games in 1896 was 10.8 feet (3.3 meters). The record is 19.42 feet (5.92 meters)—that's 80 percent higher!

UP, UP, AND AWAY

Pole vaulters use a long, bendy pole to spring over enormous jumps. As they run up to the jump, they push one end of the pole into a box that's sunk into the ground just in front of the jump. This causes the pole to bend, and by hanging on to the other end, the athletes hurl themselves up into the air.

Emma George

Sergey Bubka

BRILLIANT BUBKA

Sergey Bubka (UKR) pulled off a spectacular jump in the 1988 Olympic Games. Having knocked the bar over on his two previous attempts, he managed to leap 19.36 feet (5.9 meters) with his last jump, breaking the Olympic record and winning the gold medal. Bubka's Olympic record was broken at the last Games, but he still holds the world record with a jump of 20.14 feet (6.14 meters).

MEN'S RECORDS: WORLD: Sergey Bubka (UKR) 20.14 ft (6.14m). OLYMPIC: Galfione (FRA), Trandenkov (USSR) & Timonchik (GER) 19

POLE VAULT

At the Games in Sydney, for the first time in Olympic history, women will be allowed to compete in the pole vault—the highest and most daring jumping event!

GOING FOR GOLD

Who will become the first women's Olympic pole vault champion? One athlete to watch is Emma George from Australia. As well as being the current world record holder, she will have the added advantage of being cheered on by her home crowd!

ANIMAL OLYMPIANS

Mako sharks don't need a pole to help them jump—they've got their powerful tails! With a flick of their fins, these fearsome fish can leap more than 23 feet (7 meters) above the water. That's higher than the world record.

POLES APART

The first pole vaulters used wooden poles. Later poles were made of bamboo, which is more springy. Then, in the 1950s, aluminum poles were introduced. The latest poles are made of fiberglass, which is light and flexible but also very strong.

SHOT PUT

This event dates back to the ancient Olympic Games. The idea is to hurl a heavy ball as far as possible.

PUT IT THIS WAY

Competitors must "put" (meaning push) the shot—they are not allowed to throw it! To gain as much power as possible, they stand at the back of the throwing circle, facing the wrong way. Then, with the shot tucked against the side of their neck, they spin around. As they do so, they straighten their arm and push the heavy ball up into the air with an explosion of energy.

A raised stop board is placed along the front edge of the throwing circle. Shot putters may touch the side of the board with their feet but they must not step on top of it, even after the shot has landed.

ANIMAL OLYMPIANS

The shot put champion at the Animal Olympics is the dung beetle. Despite their small size, these little bugs collect huge balls of elephant manure to lay their eggs in. These balls can be bigger than a shot but the beetles push them around with ease!

Bernd Kneissler

Competitors must not step outside the throwing circle until the throw has been complete. The circle is 7 feet (2.1 meters) across.

The shot must land between these two white lines. If it falls outside the lines, the throw doesn't count.

WEIGH TO GO

The men's shot weighs 16.01 pounds (7.26 kg) and can be up to 5.1 inches (13 cm) across — about the same size as a grapefruit, only much heavier. The shot used by women athletes is lighter and smaller. It weighs 8.8 pounds (4 kg) and has a diameter of 4.3 inches (11 cm).

THE ROAD TO GOLD

The first thing you have to do if you want to win a gold medal in the shot put (or any of the other throwing events) is to qualify by throwing the minimum required distance. This gets you into the finals where you have three throws. If you end up in the top eight, you then get three more throws. And if you manage to throw farther than anyone else — you get the gold!

DID YOU KNOW?

In the ancient Games, competitors used a ball made of stone but the modern shot is made of metal.

Women competed in the shot put for the first time in 1948.

The first female champion was a French concert pianist named Micheline Ostermeyer, who also won gold in the discus and a bronze medal in the high jump!

DISCUS

The key to success in the discus event is a powerful but controlled throw. The launch must be smooth. If the discus wobbles, it won't fly as far.

IN A SPIN

To launch the discus with as much power as possible, the athletes spin themselves around with their arms outstretched. Here's the reigning women's Olympic champion, Ilke Wyludda (GER), showing how it's done!

DISCUS DIMENSIONS

The men's discus measures 7.8 inches (20 cm) across and weighs 4.4 pounds (2 kg), making it almost an inch (2 cm) larger and twice as heavy as the women's discus. Athletes in ancient Greece threw a discus made of solid bronze. These days, discuses are usually made of wood with a metal rim. As you can see from this picture, the discus is much fatter in the middle than around the edge.

FANTASTIC FOUR

The greatest discus thrower the Olympics has ever seen was Al Oerter (USA). He won the gold medal four times in a row between 1956 and 1968, setting an Olympic record each time. Only two other people have won four consecutive golds in the same event. One is yachtsman Paul Elvström (DEN), in the men's single-handed dinghy event.

Do you know who the other one is? You'll find the answer on page 3.

SUPER STATS

The discus is the only throwing event in which the women's records (both world and Olympic) are farther than the men's records!

Iike Wyludda

SAFETY NET

Competitors must throw the discus from a throwing circle, just like shot putters (see page 12). This circle is 8.2 feet (2.5 meters) across, making it slightly larger than the one used in other throwing events. It's surrounded on three sides by a wire cage or net, which stops the discus from being accidentally thrown toward the crowd.

DID YOU KNOW?

❦ No man has ever broken a world record in the discus at the Olympics!

❦ Competitors must not step outside the throwing circle until the discus has hit the ground. If they do, the throw will be disallowed.

❦ The ancient Greeks considered the winner of the discus to be the greatest athlete of all.

JAVELIN

This event is a spear-throwing contest. It began as part of the military training for ancient Greek soldiers!

Heli Rantanen

GET A GRIP

There are three different ways to hold a javelin. Most champions use the Finnish method. This involves gripping the javelin between your thumb and your last three fingers, with your index finger underneath it.

YOU BE THE JUDGE

For a throw to count, the javelin must land within the fan-shaped landing area at the end of the throwing area. It must also land point-first although it doesn't have to stick in the ground.

SUPER STATS

To set a world record in the men's javelin, you would have to throw it almost 328 feet (100 meters). That's more than three times the length of the longest dinosaur!

MEN'S RECORDS: WORLD: Jan Zelezny (CZE) 323.1 ft (98.48m). **OLYMPIC:** Zelezny (CZE) 294.2 ft (89.66m).

FARTHER & FARTHER

Erik Lemming (SWE) won the first Olympic javelin competition in 1906 with a throw of 176.84 feet (53.9 meters). The winning throw has gotten longer and longer. And longer! In 1976, the men's Olympic record stood at 310.3 feet (94.58 meters). In 1984, Uwe Hohn (GDR) set a world record of 343.83 feet (104.8 meters). In 1986, the javelin's design was changed.

> **Women's Olympic champ, Heli Rantanen (FIN), at the European Championships in 1988**

RECORD COLLECTION

This diagram shows how the men's Olympic javelin record has increased since 1906:

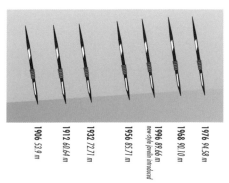

1906 53.9 m · 1912 60.64 m · 1932 72.71 m · 1956 85.71 m · 1996 89.66 m new-style javelin introduced · 1968 90.10 m · 1976 94.58 m

NEW DESIGN

The judges feared that if throws continued to improve, a javelin would one day land on the running track. So, in 1986, the design of the men's javelin was changed, making it harder to throw. The women's javelin was changed in 1999.

DID YOU KNOW?

At the ancient Olympic Games, prizes were awarded in the javelin for accuracy as well as for the greatest distance thrown.

Matti Järvinen (FIN) broke the world javelin record no fewer than 11 times between 1930 and 1936.

Javelin throwers are allowed to put resin on their hands to improve their grip, but gloves are forbidden.

MEN'S RECORDS: WORLD: Trine Hattestad (NOR) 223.72 ft (68.19m). **OLYMPIC**: P. Felke (GDR) 245.01 ft (74.68m).

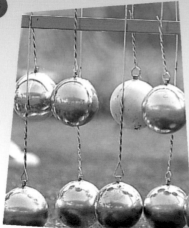

HAMMER TIME

The hammer doesn't actually look like a hammer at all. It's a metal ball attached to a strong metal wire with a handle on the end. The hammer weighs the same as the shot put—16 pounds (7.26 kg) for the men and 8.8 pounds (4 kg) for women.

DID YOU KNOW?

Hammer throwers stand in a throwing circle 7 feet (2.14 meters) across—the same size as the circle used by shot putters. Like discus throwers, they are protected by a safety net.

The United States won every single hammer competition from 1900 to 1924—but has only won the event once since then!

Although the hammer is the same weight as the shot, it can be thrown almost four times as far!

A FEMALE FIRST

Women will compete in the hammer for the first time at the Games in Sydney. The favorite for the gold is Mihaela Melinte (ROM), who is the current world record holder and reigning world champion.

SUPER STATS

The hammer used in the men's event is five times heavier than a human brain!

THE HAMMER

What does it take to be a champion hammer thrower? If you think the answer is plenty of muscle and a fine sense of balance, you've hit the nail on the head!

HOW TO DO IT

Stand at the back of the circle, facing the wrong way. Grip the handle with both hands, then swing the hammer around your head. When the hammer has gained enough momentum, spin yourself around the circle three or four times...then let go!

This picture shows Balazs Kiss (HUN), the reigning Olympic hammer champion.

WOMEN'S RECORDS: WORLD: Mihaela Melinte (ROM) 249.57 ft (76.07m). **OLYMPIC**: This will be set in Sydney.

THE HEPTATHLON

The heptathlon is for women only and combines no fewer than seven different athletic events.

BUSY DAYS

The heptathlon is contested over two days, and the seven events are always held in the same order. Day one kicks off with the 100-meter hurdles, followed by the high jump, the shot put. Day two begins with the 200 meters, long jump, the javelin, and, finally, the 800 meters.

ANIMAL OLYMPIANS

The kangaroo would certainly be able to take the heptathlon's jumping events in its stride. These powerful animals can high jump more than 10 feet (3 meters) and long jump more than 30 feet (9 meters). With a top speed of 19 mph (30 km/h), the running races should be a breeze, too, although the throwing events might not be so easy!

Ghada Shouaa

REIGNING CHAMPION

This picture of heptathlete Ghada Shouaa (SYR) was taken at the 1995 World Championships, which she won! In 1996, she picked up a gold medal at the Olympics, too.

SNICKERS
862
GÖTEBORG '95

WOMEN'S RECORDS: WORLD: Jackie Joyner-Kersee (USA) 7,291 points.

GET THE POINT?

Competitors are awarded points according to the distance, height, or time they achieve in each of the events. This means that someone who performs well in all of the events but doesn't actually win any of them will probably beat someone who wins one event but does badly in all of the others. That's why it's important to be a good all-arounder!

Jackie Joyner-Kersee

DID YOU KNOW?

The heptathlon was included in the Olympic Games for the first time in 1984.

In 1981, the heptathlon replaced the original pentathlon (not to be confused with the modern pentathlon—see page 28), which was composed of just five events.

Jackie Joyner-Kersee's late sister-in-law, the famous sprinter Florence Griffith-Joyner, won gold medals in the 100 meters, 200 meters, and 4 x 100-meter relay.

JUMPING FOR JOY-NER

Jackie Joyner-Kersee (USA) missed the gold medal by just five points at the 1984 Games. However, in 1988, she made certain to win the gold, smashing her own world record by 76 points! In 1992, she won the heptathlon for a second time and has also won one gold and two bronze medals in the long jump.

WOMEN'S RECORDS: OLYMPIC: Jackie Joyner-Kersee (USA) 7,291 points.

SHOE BUSINESS

Decathletes need at least five different pairs of shoes! A running shoe (with short spikes), a long jump shoe (with longer spikes), a high jump shoe (spikes on the heel as well as the toe), a discus and shot put shoe (no spikes), and a javelin shoe (spikes and support around the ankle).

DID YOU KNOW?

The very first Olympic decathlon held in 1904 was quite different from the modern competition. Events included throwing a 56-lb (25.55-kg) weight and an 880-yard (805-meter) walk!

In 1912, the decathlon was won by Jim Thorpe (USA), who went on to become one of America's greatest football stars.

Thorpe was later disqualified because he was a professional athlete. In 1982, 29 years after his death, members of the International Olympic Committee changed their minds and reinstated him as a gold medalist.

Daley Thompson

THE DALEY NEWS

The first decathlon was won by an athlete named Thomas Kiely (GBR) in 1904. However, Great Britain didn't win another medal in the event until 1980, when Daley Thompson won the gold. This picture of Thompson was taken on his way to a second victory at the Olympics in 1984. He still holds the Olympic record.

MEN'S RECORDS: WORLD: Tomas Dvorak (CZE) 8,994 points.

THE DECATHLON

*T**he decathlon is similar to the heptathlon, except that this competition is for men only and is made up of 10 different events.***

O'BRIEN vs. DVORAK

Dan O'Brien (USA) broke the world record in 1992 and won the gold at the 1996 Olympic Games. However, his record was broken by Tomas Dvorak (CZE). O'Brien took the news well. "I'm not disappointed," he said. "Now, I know there's somebody out there who can compete against me."

KEEP GOING

Stamina is the key to success in the decathlon. Competitors take part in 10 events in just two days — three jumps, three throws, and four races. On the first day, they tackle the 100 meters, long jump, shot put, high jump, and 400 meters, in that order. On the second day, they compete in the 110-meter hurdles, discus, pole vault, javelin, and 1,500 meters. Whew!

Decathletes need to be fast as well as strong. But even they can't sprint as quickly as a pet cat! The fastest human can run around 22 mph (35 km/h), but cats have a top speed of almost 31mph (50 km/h).

ANIMAL OLYMPIANS

Dan O' Brien

THE TRIATHLON

A new sport called the triathlon makes its first appearance at the Olympics in Sydney.

SPLASH, PEDAL, SPRINT

The triathlon is a grueling nonstop race that combines swimming, cycling, and running. The 50 athletes who start each race begin by swimming 1 mile (1.5 km), then without a rest, they jump on a bicycle and cycle another 25 miles (40 km). But the end of the bike ride isn't the end of the race. They then have to run another 6 miles (10 km) on foot to get to the finish line!

Special triathlon handlebars called tri-bars allow the cyclist to crouch very low, reducing wind resistance and allowing the bike to go faster.

SUPER STATS

The Olympic triathlon course covers 32 miles (51.5 km) in all. It would take the average tortoise about 140 hours to travel this far. Human competitors usually complete the course in around 2 hours!

The cycles used in the triathlon are lightweight racing bikes.

All competitors must wear helmets while biking.

Harrop

ULTRA TOUGH

The length of a triathlon course can vary. The toughest is known as the ultracourse. This involves a 2.4-mile (3.8-km) swim, a 112-mile (180-km) cycle ride (often through the mountains), and a 26-mile (42-km) run. The best competitors finish it in about 8 hours!

Each competitor has a number. If there isn't room for the number on their clothes, athletes write it on their skin.

DID YOU KNOW?

Competitors are allowed to change their clothes at the end of each stage.

The biggest triathlon event took place in Chicago in 1987. Exactly 3,888 people started the event — but you can bet that not all of them managed to finish it!

Doctors and medical teams are on hand at every stage of the competition to check the athletes' condition.

IRONMEN & WOMEN

The triathlon was invented by U. S. servicemen stationed in Hawaii about 25 years ago. They came up with the grueling competition as a way of testing their fitness. They called it the Ironman race. However, triathletes such as Jackie Gallagher (AUS) and Loretta Harrop (AUS) have proven that there are Ironwomen out there, too. Both are strong contenders for a medal at Sydney.

Jackie Gallagher

Each course is different in each venue, so times are not compared.

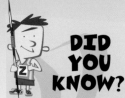

DID YOU KNOW?

⟫ Triathletes wear padded shorts to prevent them from getting blisters on their bottom during the cycling event!

⟫ The first official triathlon competition was held in 1978.

⟫ The triathlon is one of only two sports making their Olympic debuts. The other newcomer is taekwondo.

TEMPERATURE CHECK

If the competitors are swimming in the sea (as they will be in Sydney), they are allowed to wear wetsuits, but only if the temperature is below 73°F (23°C). If the water is above this temperature, they must wear only swimsuits!

Hamish Carter

HEADSTRONG

Mental strength is just as important as physical strength in the triathlon. As well as being incredibly fit, competitors need an iron-strong will to make themselves keep going through each of the three exhausting stages.

Sydney Opera House

NICE VIEW

The swimming race will be held in the world-famous Sydney Harbour. This should give the athletes a great view of two of Australia's most famous landmarks—the Sydney Harbour Bridge and the Sydney Opera House. Not that they will have much time to admire the scenery!

THE TRIATHLON
(CONTINUED)

The triathlon is considered the toughest Olympic event of them all—although decathletes might disagree!

ANIMAL OLYMPIANS

Even triathletes are slow swimmers when compared to fish. Humans have a top speed in the water of about 5 mph (8 km/h), but most fish can swim at least three times as fast.

MEDAL CONTENDERS

New Zealand's top triathlete, Hamish Carter, was ranked number 1 in the world during 1999. He has an excellent chance of winning gold at the Games in 2000. However, he can expect some stiff competition from the reigning World Champion Simon Lessing (GBR) and Dmitriy Gaag (KAZ), among others.

THE MODERN PENTATHLON

T he five events of the modern pentathlon are inspired by the legend of a courageous French soldier in the nineteenth century who was sent to deliver a message.

STORY TIME

According to the legend, the soldier set off on horseback, riding as fast as he could across the rough terrain (**SHOWJUMPING**). After a while, he came across an enemy soldier, who challenged him to a duel. The messenger drew his sword and won the duel (**FENCING**). As he went to get back on his horse, he heard a gunshot. The bullet missed the messenger but killed his poor horse. Quick as a flash, the soldier pulled out his pistol and returned fire (**SHOOTING**). He then swam across a raging river (**200-METER FREESTYLE**) before running the rest of the way (**3,000 METERS**) and finally delivering his message.

SUPER STATS

2ND 1ST 3RD

Sweden dominated the men's individual pentathlon for more than 50 years, winning gold in this event at 9 out of the 12 games between 1912 and 1968! Hungary is second with four golds, and Poland is third with two.

Pierre de Coubertin

MODERN BEGINNINGS

The modern pentathlon has been part of the Games since 1912. It was introduced by a Frenchman named Pierre de Coubertin. Often called "the father of the Olympics," Coubertin was also responsible for organizing the first modern Games in 1896, and he was the first president of the International Olympic Committee.

ANCIENT ORIGINS

The Greeks came up with the idea of combining five different events in one competition. The first recorded pentathlon was held at the ancient Olympic Games in 708 B. C. It included jumping, running, the discus throw, the javelin throw, and wrestling.

Tomas Fleissner (CZE)

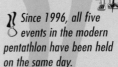

DID YOU KNOW?

♫ Since 1996, all five events in the modern pentathlon have been held on the same day.

♫ George Patton (USA), who came in fifth in the pentathlon in 1912, went on to become one of the most famous American generals of World War II, despite the fact that he did poorly in the shooting event!

♫ As well as the individual competition, there used to be a team event in the modern pentathlon. This was held for the last time in 1992.

DID YOU KNOW?

)} At the 1936 Games, Charles Leonard (USA) scored 200 points in the shooting event. That is the highest possible score.

)} Leonard's remarkable achievement was matched in 1980 by a sharpshooting Swedish pentathlete named George Horvath.

)} Paul Lednev (URS) won a record seven Olympic medals in the modern pentathlon between 1968 and 1980 —four in the individual competition and three in the team event.

WHAT A CHEATER!

One of the worst Olympic scandals ever occurred during the 1976 Games, when one of the Soviet pentathletes was caught cheating. Judges discovered that Boris Onischenko (URS) had tampered with the sword he was using in the fencing event so that it registered a hit even if he missed his opponent!

LADIES FIRST

The modern pentathlon is another Olympic event in which women will be able to compete for the first time in Sydney. Keep an eye out for Anna Sulima and Paulina Boenisz (POL), Janna Dolgacheva-Shubenok (BLR), and Fabiana Fares (ITA), as all four athletes are expected to do well.

Daniel Massala (ITA)

Graham Bookhouse (GBR)

SHOOTING STARS

In the shooting event, competitors fire 2(shots at a target that is about 33 feet (10 meters) away. They are given just 40 seconds to fire each shot. Originally competitors shot with a rapid-fire pistol, but since 1996, they have used an air pist(

THE MODERN PENTATHLON
(CONTINUED)

Versatility is the key to success in the modern pentathlon. Each of the events requires very different skills.

SADDLE UP

The showjumping course in the modern pentathlon is around 400 meters long and consists of 12 different jumps. Points are awarded to each competitor according to the time taken to complete the course. However, competitors lose points for knocking down an obstacle.

SUPER STATS

The jumps in the modern pentathlon's equestrian event are as much as 4 feet (130 cm) high—that's taller than an average 8-year-old!

INDEX

Acknowledgments

We would like to thank Ian Hodge, Rosalind Beckman, Jackie Gaff, and Elizabeth Wiggans for their assistance. Cartoons by John Alston.

Copyright © 2000 *ticktock* Publishing Ltd.

First published in Great Britain by ticktock Publishing Ltd., The Offices in the Square, Hadlow, Tonbridge, Kent TN11 0DD, Great Britain.

Printed in Hong Kong.

Picture Credits: All images from (c) Allsport. Picture research by Image Select.

Library of Congress Cataloging-in-Publication Data

Page, Jason.
    Athletics, Field : pole vault, long jump, hammer, javelin, and lots, lots more / by Jason Page.
        p. cm. -- (Zeke's Olympic pocket guide)
    Includes index.
    Summary: Describes the field events of the Olympic Games and previews the field events for the 2000 Olympic Games.
    ISBN 0-8225-5053-9 (alk. paper)
    1. Track-athletics--Juvenile literature. 2. Olympics--Juvenile literature. [1. Track and field. 2. Olympics.] I. Title. II. Series.
GV1060.5 .P24 2000
796.43--dc21
                                                                                    00-008098